Adult
ABCs

Plus

SINS

7 DEADLY

7 NOT QUITE SO DEADLY

Poems and Illustrations by

Elizabeth McBride Smith

Speed Bump Press

This book was designed, written and illustrated by
Elizabeth McBride Smith

Published by

Speed Bump Press
Corralitos, California

Printed on acid-free recycled paper by
Dave Parker at Harbor Press,
in Santa Cruz, California

For additional copies, contact the author at:

speedbumppress@myway.com

For

Carrie and Aaron

CONTENTS

ABCs   **1-28**

A	3
B	4
C	5
D	6
E	7
F	8
G	9
H	10
I	11
J	12
K	13
L	14
M	15
N	16
O	17
P	18
Q	19
R	20
S	21
T	22
U	23
V	24
W	25
X	26
Y	27
Z	28

CONTENTS

SINS   29

Wrath   31

Deception   32

Gluttony   33

Gossips   34

Greed   35

Ignorance   36

Indifference   37

Selfishness   38

Envy   39

Lust   40

Vanity   41

Sloth   42

Pride   43

Sadism   44

Acknowledgements   47

About The Author   48

ABCs

A

Ageing Adelaide, Adjusting her dentures

Answered an Ad for some big time Adventures

Artfully Adjusting her hair and Attire

Admired herself and to love did Aspire

On the Attack, new love to Attract

Assessed her Amount of Allure, but

Fear of becoming An Audacious tart
Made her a little unsure

She Assumed that Affection from many directions

Would Amuse her Along the way, then Addressed her

Afflictions and Astounding Addictions

And Admirably called it A day

B

Old Biddies' Birthdays are Better with Buddies

From Birth to our Bailouts and all in-Between

Bummers and Blunders and Blisses and Blessings

Bereavements and Bye-Byes and Bannered Beginnings

So Bite the Bad Bullet

And Bring on the Band

While over and over we'll
Make our last stand

C

A Classic Case

A Crusade

A Cult of Craven Crones

Carousing to Crazy Cadences of Caustic Cacophony

Culminating in Choruses of Carelessly Concocted

Chilling Combinations of

Creaking Cursing Cellos and Complaining Clarinets

Creating a Calamitous Careening Clatter

A Clink

A Clang

A Crash of Chords

Crudely Conceived in Chaos

A Concert Cursed Complete with Ceremony

Contrived to Conquer all the Contentment the

Cosmos now Contains

D

D is for Dorothy
Debra and Drew
Dating and Dumping as
Debutantes do
    so
Devoted to Dalliance
Discreet and Designing
Dreaming of Diamonds sweet
Damsels Divining
    but
Dynamos, Dawdlers
Dandies and Dudes
Damage their Dreams and
Damsels Delude

E

The Emperor and Empress of an Excellent domain
Enslaved Enormous Elephants to Enjoy and Entertain the
Entourage of Elders and Eventually obtain
Their Everlasting gratitude and Eliminate disdain
Emblazoned Eagles, numbered Eight, Encircled daily this Estate
Exquisite Egrets would Enhance the Evening with their lovely dance

Eventually the Elephants all made their Escape
The Eagles and the Egrets fled and I have often heard it said
In Exile, Elders, Extinct or dead
To an Everlasting Eden fled

F

Ferdy and Freddie had a
Fling at Fine Fashion, but
Foretelling of Fame was
Foolish and Frail
In Fact they were Frizzled and
Frumpy and Frazzled, with no
Flair For the Future
Forewarning they'd Fail
Fancies of Fame Flashed
Forever before them, but in a
Frightening Funk they knew they were done
Then
Finding Fine Friends of Failure Forgiving
They gave Fame the Finger
In Favor of Fun

G

Glimpses and Guesses are my Galaxy Guides

Gazing at Gathering stars far and wide

To Grasp all the Grandeur, the Gleam and the Glow

To contemplate God from this side 'till I know

I'll Go mad with the Gollys and mad with the Gees

Then I'll Get me some Grapes and a small bit of cheese

I'll be Gratful for Generous Goblets of wine

And think about Glory some other time

H

Hi Ho to Hamlet, Hearing Pop's voice
Hurt and Heroic, Hassled a choice
Hot with His Hormones, Heavy with Hate
Hassled an Honorable, internal debate

Hostile to Heroine, Humble and sweet
Hampered by Honor he plays Hide and seek
Hapless and Helpless, Hopeful but Hurt, she
Hastens the Horror by becoming inert

Hail and Hardy, our Hamlet, not Hostile to Hope
Hungry to prove He's no longer a dope
Hedging his bets and Hacking away

Proved playing Shakespeare's no roll in the Hay

I

If Icarus, with Impunity, did fly to

Incandescence, as he was Inclined

Imperiled with Impending Immolation

Impetuously Inspired to Illuminate his

Island sky, was found Inverted In the salty sea

Indeed on Impact was Imperiled but proved

Inviolate, Immune to Injury, as If

Insouciant Gods did Interfere to

Insure Invulnerability to Immediate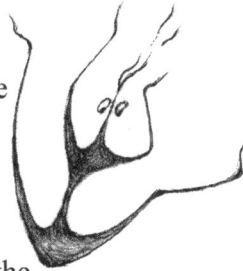

Immolation, Ah, how to Impose

Indulgence In an Inconsistent tale

I would Invent, Inspired solely by the

Intriguing and Impelling and

Impressive letter I

J

Jacob, Jason, Joseph and John
Jazzed with the Jargon
Jammed with the Jive, Just
Jetsetting Jesters, but
Jiggled Alive, by

Jenny, Jasmine, Julie and Jean, who
Journeyed to Jersey, all
Jaunty with Jest, to spring them from
Jail, they were under arrest

The Judge and the Jury found
Joints in their Jeans, said
Jumping Jehospahats, they're
Still in their teens

Jacob, Jason, Joseph and John
Jumped bail for Jamaica
This is no Jest
Jumped bail for the girls

You can figure the rest

K

Kathleen and Katherine, everyone Knew, from
Kabul to Kansas to Kalamazoo, liked a
   Kiss in the Kitchen, Kinky or Kosher, but
Kept their Karate reserved for the grocer
   Kenneth and Karl picked up the Key and
Kings of Karate pretended to be, then a
   Kick to the Kidney and a Knock to the
Knee soon let the girls Know how
   Kinky they'd be. No Kudos, those
Kiddos were Princes of Klutz
   Kaput as good lovers, no ifs, ands or buts, so they
Knowingly Kept them as Kith and as Kin to
   Kindle some Kindness when Karma wore thin

L

Languid Lydia Lay upon her
Lovely Lounge all Lace and Lily Like
Love, she Lied, has Laid me Low with
Longing so

Lean Lecherous Leonard, a
Lowland Lout who Little Loved but
Likely Lived a Lot
Leapt and Landed Lightly on the
Lovely Limbs of Lydia

Luck did Loom, for Lydia
Liked the Leaping
Lad she Lured, and 'neath him
Longed to Learn, but while
Listening to the Litany of
Lovers she had Lost
Leonard's Lack of Lust made
Leonard Late so
Leonard Left

M

Merry Music the Marvelous Maidens Make
Measure for Measure Making no Mistake
Meanwhile Missing Much Mischievous fun, the
Men March off to Mayhem's Murderous drum
More Military Madness to be done

Mirthlessly Moralizing this Malaise Must
Mask the Mindless way we Misbehave, while
Merriment Makes Minister to Mock all
Misadventure, and take stock of
Memory's Morbid Melancholy lot

N

Numerous Nymphos, both Naughty and Nice
Necked and Nimble and Noisy with vice

Next are the Nuisances, Ninnies and Nerds
Needing Narcotics with Needles, how weird

Numberless, Nameless ones, Numb with Neglect
Never are Nurtured and receive No respect

Negative Nurses and Nagging Nuns, from
Noontime to Nighttime leaving Novices glum

Never Neurotic, the Neutral, the Nice, always
Near when you Need them, No traumas, No vice

Neat Notions of Normal, Notoriously Naive
Nappy with Nonsense, should Not be believed

O

Olivia Obligingly Offered hors d'Oeuvres

Oliver Ordered them not to be served

Onions and Olives in Over-sweet Oil

Off-color Oysters too long in the boil

Organs of Owl, and Offal of Ox

Nothing you'd want to take home in a box

Oceans Of Octopus, an Oddity Odious

Organs Of Ostrich in helpings commodious

Organic Okra, Oblong and Oozing

Oranges plus Opium, An Offer Outstanding

Outrageous Occasion, Oppressively grounding

P

Prince or Pauper

Professor or Punk

Publish or Perish

Palace or dump

Priest or Pagan

Pray or Perform

Penitence or Pleasure

Piety or Porn

Plain or Preposterous

Proud or Profane

Pity the People

Perusing their Pain

Picking Pursuits

Phonic or Physical

Punished with Platitudes

Pure or Political

Q

Querulous Quincy, a Quibbling Queen
Quoted a Quip from a Quack
Quadruple the Quinine a
Quart to Quell Quaking and
Quicken a Quant to his back

R

The Reverent Ruth Recoiled
From her Randy Risqué Rhymes
And all the Restless Rowdiness
Toward which she was inclined
All the Ribald Rhapsodies and
Reeling Roundelays could Not
Reverse, could not Reroute
Her Reluctant better days

Rallied was her Rare Restraint
But Rigid were her Rules
To Reconstruct and Reconcile
A nature that was dual
To Rigors such could we Relate
Or Rewards to one Reclaimed
Who Resisted and did not Resent that

She'd become Restrained
Ruth, Righteous now and Rescued
In her crown, another thorn
Resolved to Revel in the Right
To be Rendered soon Reborn
Rejoicingly Rerouted and
Rapturously Redeemed, she's
Robbed of Reason, Robbed of Rights
Regretting her Regime

S

A Softened Sliver of Savory Shrimp Slid Silently down her chin
She Salvaged a bit upon her lip and Safely guided it in
A Sordid Scene, it did demean a lady So Sedate, So She
Settled for Sauce, gave it a toss and

Decided to use a plate

T

With a bang and a Twang and a
Tit for a Tat, Triple Time Trevor
Tried a Tune in his hat
With a Tra and a la and a Trounce and a splat
A Twelve Tone Transcending Tradition
Went flat

Toots on the Tuba with Tedium Teeming
The Tympani's Timber with Temperament
Streaming
With Tempo most Temporal, Tenaciously Tending
We Thought That This Turkey

Would never be ending

U

Uncle was a Unicorn
Unsure and Under Stress
Uneasy that the Universe was
Undefined at best

    Undaunted by his single horn, my
    Uncle was a Unicorn

Understanding Unity
Unsure and Unavailable, he
Urgently sought Utopia
Undelivered, Unattainable

    Undaunted by his single horn my
    Uncle was a Unicorn

V

Various Visits from the Virile
Vulgar Vicar Vexed the
Vain and Valiant Vestal Virgins
Verily, his Vast and Vaunted Visage hoped to
Vanquish Vital Values, Various and Vague

Vile Villainy they Vehemently Voiced,
Vanquish not our Virtue but
Validate, not Violate our Vows

We may be

Virtual Volcanos of Voluptuousness
Velvet Voiced and Vulnerable, but our
Verticality must be Victorious

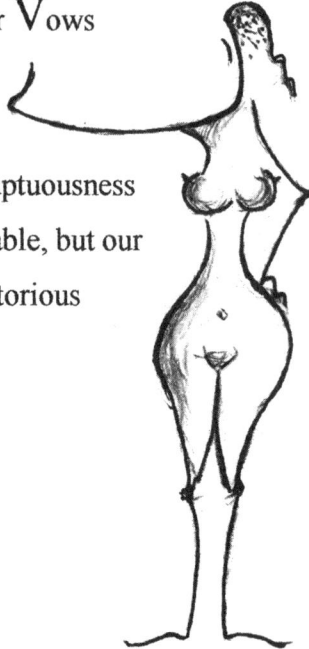

W

Winnie, Wantonly, Wickedly Willing

Winters With Wallis and

Wanders With Willie

Winnie Wants Wallis When

Willie is Working but

Winnie Wants Willie When

Wallis is Worn

Willie Wrote Wallis that

Winnie Was Wanton and

Wallis Wrote Willie that

Winnie Was Worse, so

Wallis he Wandered and

Willie he Wavered and

Wretched With Weeping

Winnie she Wondered if

Welcoming Waldo and

Wandering With Willard Would _____

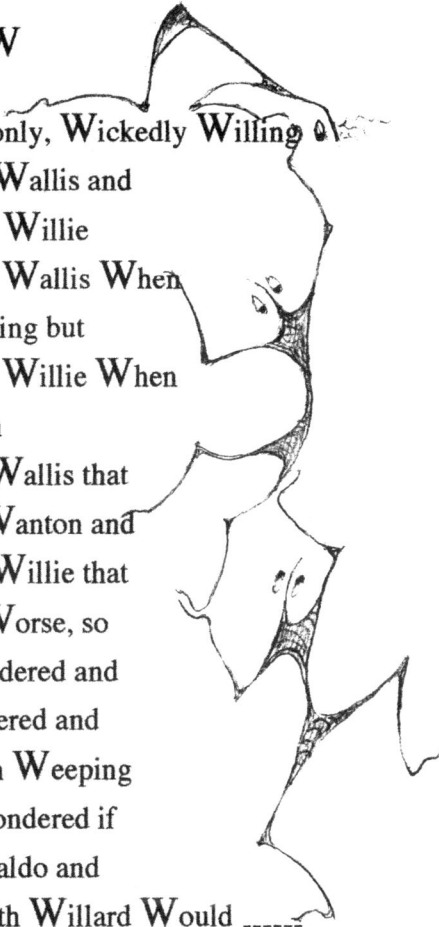

X

I would eXpect my eXceptionally eXquisite and
eXotic eXterior eXtremities to eXcite eXploration of an
eXemplary nature
The eXtended eXcitement should
eXpress the eXtremes of eXpressive and eXpansive eXuberance.

Y

A Yogi from Yemen and a Yankee from Yale
Picked up a Yacht and set a tall sail
She was Yar but her Yaw made them wonder
If they'd soon make the Yukon or Yield to the Yonder
The Yogi confused his Yang with his Yin and
Soon they would know the trouble they're in

The Yeoman, no Yahoo, nor YoYo, but Yank
Took up the oar and went for the bank
They picked up a Yenta who would show them the way
Wise but still Young, she could hold them in sway
So off to the rivers that started with Y

It would take a few years but they'd gave it a try
The Yana, the Yakima, Yalung and Yozoo
The Yenisei, the Yangtze and Yata would do
It wasn't the Yukon, they sailed far off the track
But no Yawn of a Yarn if they ever got back

Z

A Zany Zoned out Zebra

Played a Zither in Zaire

The Zoo is not for me he said,
As we all stood up to cheer

He played with Zeal of Zionists,

He played with Zest of Zen,

When he'd played for half a day
He played it all again.

With great Zoom he filled the room

And at the Zenith of his joy,

He Zeroed out and lost his clout

His Zig all Zaged, poor boy

SINS

W rath

War's Wrath Widens the Wedge
that Weakens and Worries
the Weary World of Woe,
Where Woman Weep
for Wrongful Widowing and
Watch and Warn of the Ways
the Wondering earth does
Weave and Wither With its Wounds
and shall bear Witness to the
Wretched Waste and Willful Wrongs

Deception

Dibs on Dicey, Ditsy Dames,
Dabbling Daily in Devious games

Determined Dangerously to Deceive
Dissembling Damsels, I believe, would

Drop me Dizzy with Delight, and
Defuse the Danger the of the night

Deft Devotees of Drink and Dance
Derail my Duty to romance

Disturb now Darkly my Desire
Dissed, but Dismissed from Devil's fire

Draw the Drape in Duped Delight
Desert me, but first Dim the light

Gluttony

Greta Gorged Grandly in a Glassy-eyed Glaze and
Gratefully Guzzled through a
Guilt-ridden haze, while
Groaning with Grits and
Gravy she Gazed toward a
Gourmand's fate in a
Godless Grave, then
Gave up the Ghost
Gasped her last and

All the rest I guess

Is Gas

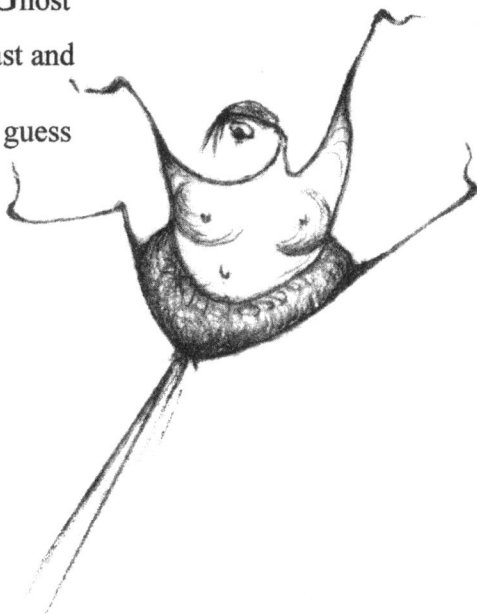

The Gossips

They Gab and they Gossip and Gladly will Grant
A Glimpse of their Grumbles, a share of their rant
The Goal is to Gloat, all Giddy with Glee
They're the Gurus of Gossip, the bitching hour three.
Glad to be Grousing, Gorging with Gall, they
Gang in a Group for telling it all
That Gertrude is Grumpy, that Gina is Gross
Their Gowns are just Ghastly, like Glue spread on toast
Good God, they Go on as they Grin and they Guess
Convinced that their friends are a Grievous mess
George has Gone whoring, he's left home for Good
His wife has Gained weight, claims she's misunderstood
Now snapping her Garters for an un-Grateful louse
She questions her Gender and Gives up the house
The Gossips are Gathered, don't open the Gate, or a
Garden of Garbage will land on your plate

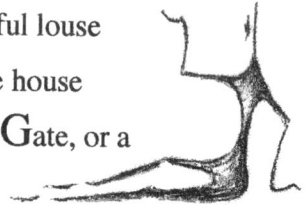

Greed

Would God could Grant that I could get
While all the Godless Getting's Good
Grasp and Gratify and Grab
As Guiltless as a piece of wood
Gasping with Galactic Groans
Gathering Gems, those Gleaming stones
A Granting of Goods to make me Gasp
Guided to my Greedy Grasp
A Gorgeous Glut of Goodies Glazed
To Gather and Guard till eyes are dazed
The Gospel of Greed would cast its spell

Then I would Gladly go to hell

Ignorance

I live In Idiot's delight
In Ignorance most Indelible
What bulb Illumes my little night
Is Insistently untenable

I don't Inspire
I don't Inquire
Indifferent to Intent
I thrive, an Ignoramus
In my Idle merriment

Innocent of thought am I
While Indomitable I reign
An Innocuous Independent
With an Imperfect Idle brain

Indifference

I have no Interest In being Involved
I'm Indifferent to problems remaining unsolved
Illusive and Idle and hard to Inspire
I seldom Inflame and never take fire

I Icely Insist that you never Invade
The Inflated Illusions I never would trade for
Interesting Issues that Inspire your Ilk
and The fine Institutions you manage to bilk

When you're Ill, Indisposed, I'm just not Impressed
I run from Infection, Ignoble at best
My Instincts Incline me to caring for none
Good Intentions, Inquiry, I Idly shun

Here's to an Icon, Impervious to fun
Invested in nothing, beholden to none

Selfishness

Sharing doesn't Suit my Style
I Seldom let things Slip away
Saving Stuff Sure makes me Smile
My Solid Stash is here to Stay

What's mine is mine! It Seems a Shame
To Sometimes give a Silver coin
A Simple Smile is more my Style
Sounds Silly, but true all the Same

You may Stand Shivering in a Storm
My Shirt Stays here Secure
The Snow may Settle on your Skin
You Shall Suffer, that's for Sure

My eyes will Shut, refuse to See you
Stager, Slide and Slip and Sway
Life's Slopes are Steep, you Seldom Sleep
Only Slender Sighs I Spare that day

Envy

Evelyn Envies Edith, Edith Envies Earl
Earl Envies dear Elizabeth and wants to be a girl
Eugene Exudes Elegance, Emma wants the same and
Elevates her small Estate to Everyone's disdain
Ethel, who has lost her chance, still, Every day
Expects to dance as well as Dell who does Excel in
Entertaining very well, now Ethel feels she lives in hell

Egos that have gone astray
Eclipse the fun of every day

Lust

I Live a Life of Leisure
The Lazy Liberty of Lust
Luring Lovely Ladies
Laved in Lavender and musk
Lean and Low my credo
A Lithe and Lusty buck
With a Lively Loose Libido
And more than a Little Luck.
Legend my Lance and Limber
In Love it Lingers Long
I'm a Libertine with Lingo
And a Larkish Lyric song, so
Light the Light for Lusty Lad:
Who with young Ladies sup
I carried one across the line
For this they Locked me up

Vanity

I Vent with Vehement Vigor
On my Various Venial sins
With Vanity I Venture forth
On Vague and Various whims

Verging on Vain glory
With Verve I wish to Vamp
The Verdict is I'm handsome
For a Vulgar Visage can't

Impress the Virtuous ladies
So Vivacious, sweet and kind
No Villain's face can keep the pace
I'm Vain, but I don't mind

Sloth

I Seek the Sedentary life
Singing Softly to Save my breath
Slipped into Sleep while
Starry Skies give way to Sun
Me, Still at rest

Sitting Sated and well Served
I Scorn the Sage, I Scorn the Saint
Submerged I Sink in Sordid Sprawl
Shabby, but with no complaint

A Squalid Specter, Septic, Sour
Without a Shred of Shame
A Sleazy Slug, to Sloth a Slave, but
Stressed with choice I'd Stay the Same

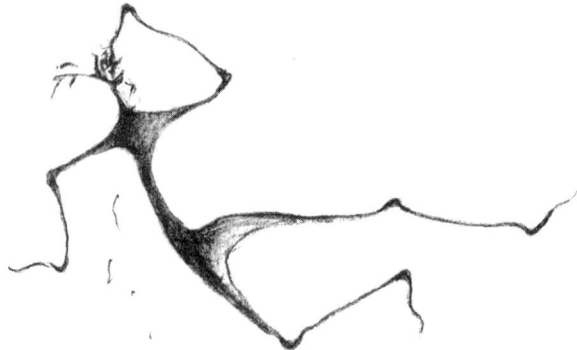

Pride

Prickly Pride is a Perilous ride
Prophetic of Power gone Puff
Propped up and Pitiful
Pretentious and critical
High on a Perch
Peering down with a huff
Pagans or Pious ones
Pretending they're Paragons
Presumptuously Painful

Via the butt

Sadism

Soft, Sweet and Simple She Seemed to be
As She Sang her Song of Compassion, but
Sylvia knew She was really a Shrew who
Would Stretch all your Sinews in traction

Satanic and Sassy, off on a Spree She
Surpassed the best in her Sport
With the Strongest of pleasure She'd then
Take her measure of Sobs she was Soon to report.

She Sang to her Siblings a Silver-tongued Spell
Then Slapped them all Soundly to Sleep
Slipped off their covers, opened the Sash and
Smiled while they Shivered, the creep

She Silenced her Sister and gave her a blister
Where blisters Seldom are Seen
Shouldered a whip, Sailed away on a Ship
Seduced Sailors who once were Serene

Nothing is Sacred, nothing is Safe
From a Sadist who's off on a Spree
She can Sicken your Soul and take Such a toll
That a Shambles is what you will be

Stay clear and Stay far, have nothing to Say
For no Secret is Safe from report
Develop a Stutter when words you would utter
And Split from the Scene, or it's *mort!*

Acknowledgements

Bonnie Quan,
who gave unstintingly of friendship, time and
energy, to teach and guide me through the making
of this book.

Helen Slater,
for the continuing encouragement and
consistent appreciation that kept me going.

Beverly Kenville,
who was a critical reader and saw me through the
buying and using of my first computer.

Melville McBride,
For the book title.

Jim Kasdorf and **Kathleen Nitz**,
For general advice and fine-tuning my spelling.

Thank you

photo by Dr. Frederick Smith

About The Author

Betty Smith lives and works.
More biographical material can be obtained,
but with great difficulty.